Sermonettes from Sebastian

A Dog's Advice on Relationship with The Master

Sermonettes from Sebastian

A Dog's Advice on Relationship with The Master

By Laura Jewell Tyree

Illustrations by Elizabeth Backlund

Eden Reign Publishing, Colorado Springs

Sermonettes from Sebastian: A Dog's Advice on Relationship with The Master
Published by Eden Reign Publishing, LLC
In connection with Eden Reign Ministries
ISBN 978-1-938030-00-0

CONTENTS

DEDICATION & ACKNOWLEDGMENTS

In loving memory of our dog-baby, Sebastian, whom we love, miss, and fully expect to be waiting to greet us in heaven!

Thank you to our Father God, Lord and Savior Jesus, and Holy Spirit, for EVERYTHING ~ in particular, for illustrating these lessons through our relationship with Sebastian and for inspiring this book!

Thank you to my parents, Fred and Alice Jewell, for your love and faithfulness to the Lord, to each other, and to our family. Thank you for your commitment to keeping God in the center of your lives and to raising your children to know, love, and serve Him. Thank you for making room for Sebastian in your hearts and home even when you thought your days of having pets were over. And thank you for all your help, encouragement and support throughout the process of writing, editing, researching and publishing. We love you!

Thank you to my precious husband, Jesse, for sharing in this great adventure of life. Thank you for being an extension of the Lord's love to me, His steadfastness, peace and comfort in the storms, and His friendship, encouragement, and joy at all times. Thank you for your constant help and support throughout the process of writing, editing, researching and publishing. I love you!

Thanks to my siblings, Terri, Jeff, and Jason, and their families for their love and support of us and Sebastian, and to Terri and Steve for helping review the book in the beginning of the process. Thanks to the Bennetts, Richardsons, and Jason and Vickie for your role in caring for Sebastian in his early life. Thanks to Liz Backlund for all your hard work to capture Sebastian in these beautiful illustrations and to help bring the book to life. And thanks to all who knew and loved Sebastian and welcomed him into your hearts and lives.

INTRODUCTION

*Your love, O LORD, reaches to the heavens, your faithfulness to the skies.
Your righteousness is like the mighty mountains, your justice like the great deep.
O LORD, you preserve both man and beast. How priceless is your unfailing love!
Both high and low among men find refuge in the shadow of your wings. They feast
on the abundance of your house; you give them drink from your river of delights.
For with you is the fountain of life; in your light we see light. Continue your love
to those who know you, your righteousness to the upright in heart.*

Psalm 36:5-10 NIV

How much does God care about you? Does He know you personally and intimately? Does He care about your struggles? Is He able to deliver you from them? Is He willing? What if I told you that God even cares for your pets and knows them by name? Would you have more faith to believe in God's love and care for you if you knew that He even loves and cares about your dog?

Sebastian is my parents' pride and joy. My siblings and I have often joked that he is the favored "child" that our Dad loves more than the rest of us. One Monday night as my husband, Jesse, and I were having our normal prayer time together, my prayer was suddenly interrupted by the thought that I needed to pray for Sebastian! Though we try to be sensitive to God's leading, this was the first time I had ever felt prompted out of the blue to pray for a dog. I stopped mid-prayer to tell Jesse what I was feeling; he responded very supportively…by laughing at me. I attempted to push the notion aside and return to what I had previously been praying, but the thought was so persistent that I could have no peace until I prayed for him. So despite my husband's amusement, I prayed for Sebastian.

That weekend we went to visit my parents in Arkansas. During dinner the first night we were there, they entertained us with stories about Sebastian's latest antics. Most of these accounts were cute and amusing, but the mood shifted as they began to relate a frightening incident from earlier that week. Dad had let Sebastian out one last time before bed, unaware of an approaching storm. Minutes later, a loud clap of thunder and the sound of pounding rain sent Mom scurrying to let Sebastian back inside ~ but he was nowhere in sight. After a fruitless search of the house, she stepped outside and, to her dismay, discovered the gate swinging open and shut in the wind. Without delay, no time to even change their clothes, my parents sprang into action, Dad in the car and Mom on foot, for a search and rescue mission around the neighborhood. Knowing Sebastian suffered from a terrible case of cowardice, they figured the thunder so terrified him that he was just running wild, not realizing what he was doing or where he was going. After twenty minutes of searching, completely circling the block, knocking on several neighbors' doors to enlist their help, and even calling the police, Mom turned to see a white blur shoot across the intersection a block away. The blur was sprinting toward the busiest street in town with only one block to spare!

As Jesse and I listened to this story, our foreknowledge that Sebastian had survived the ordeal lessened the suspense and anxiety we might have otherwise felt, so I was momentarily more "sympathetically" focused on the image of my Mom wandering the street in her nightgown and raincoat in a storm, at 11:00 p.m., shouting Sebastian's name. Just as I was thinking, 'Oh No! My parents have become *those people*" in the neighborhood,' the Lord jolted me out of my *compassionate sensitivity* for the plight my parents had endured by reminding me of our prayer for Sebastian.

Immediately I blurted out, "WHAT NIGHT WAS THIS?!" When they responded, "Monday," I looked at Jesse, eyes wide and mouth gaping and exclaimed, "That's the night we prayed for Sebastian!" We excitedly told them what had happened in our prayer time. Surprised, my parents inquired, "What did you pray?!" So I recounted my simple request, "God I don't know why You have put Sebastian on my heart, but I pray that You bless him and protect him. I ask that You give him a long life because he has been such a blessing to my parents and has brought them so much joy."

When we compared notes, we realized that their fiasco had taken place at the exact time we were praying! After expressing their amazement, Mom concluded the story, telling how she had screamed Sebastian's name just as the white blur shot out of sight, racing toward the busy street ahead. A moment later, it reappeared, rounded the corner, and sprinted toward home! It WAS Sebastian! Mom turned just the right direction at just the right time and yelled just loud enough over the rain and noisy street ahead…by coincidence, right? Not a chance! Though Mom says it would have been miraculous even if Sebastian heard her, I like to imagine there was a huge angel blocking his path as he took his final steps toward Race Street which startled him even more than the storm had, causing him to turn tail and bolt back the other way. Regardless of how He accomplished it, the fact remains that Sebastian's well being was important to God. He had prompted me to pray for Sebastian at the very moment of his crisis, and through our prayer God intervened in the circumstances to rescue him!

Since Sebastian experienced the Lord's divine deliverance, out of profound gratitude he has dedicated his life to encouraging others to find a deeper relationship with God through sharing life lessons on relationship with the Master. (For those who suspect Sebastian may have had some help writing, read on.)

This book was birthed the following summer, 2005, when Jesse and I hosted Sebastian while my parents were in Finland doing mission work. He was a blessing from the Lord, bringing joy and laughter during what was otherwise a very challenging season for us. Through our experiences with Sebastian in those months, God spoke to us often, showing us parallels that sweetly and humorously illustrated His love for us and our relationship with Him.

My prayer is that the lessons God demonstrated through our relationship with Sebastian will bless and encourage you in your relationship with THE MASTER as well, and that you will know with absolute certainty that if God loves and cares individually for every animal, He loves and cares for you EVEN MORE!

(Story in the introduction corresponds to pages 61-64.)

Therefore I tell you, do not worry about your life, what you will eat or drink; or about your body, what you will wear. Is not life more important than food, and the body more important than clothes? Look at the birds of the air; they do not sow or reap or store away in barns, and yet your heavenly Father feeds them. Are you not of much more value than they? Who of you by worrying can add a single hour to his life? And why do you worry about clothes? See how the lilies of the field grow. They do not labor or spin. Yet I tell you that not even Solomon in all his splendor was dressed like one of these. If that is how God clothes the grass of the field, which is here today and tomorrow is thrown into the fire, will he not much more clothe you, O you of little faith? So do not worry, saying, "What shall we eat?" or "What shall we drink?" or "What shall we wear?" For the pagans run after all these things, and your heavenly Father knows that you need them. But seek first his kingdom and his righteousness, and all these things will be given to you as well.

Matthew 6:25-33 NIV

Are not five sparrows sold for two pennies? Yet not one of them is forgotten by God. Indeed, the very hairs on your head are all numbered. Don't be afraid; you are worth more than many sparrows.

Luke 12:6-7 NIV

ALONG FOR THE RIDE

If the Master is going somewhere, always be ready to go with Him.

"Come, follow me," Jesus said, "and I will make you fishers of men."

Matthew 4:19 NIV

You don't have to know where you're going; if the Master is driving, just enjoy the ride.

Trust in the LORD with all your heart; do not depend
on your own understanding. Seek his will in all you
do, and he will show you which path to take.

Proverbs 3:5-6 NLT

The road may be bumpy and the trip may be long, but it's better to be with the Master in discomfort than in a comfortable spot without Him.

One day spent in your house, this beautiful place of worship, beats thousands spent on Greek island beaches. I'd rather scrub floors in the house of my God than be honored as a guest in the palace of sin.

Psalm 84:10 MSG

No matter how long you've been on the journey, never stop watching out for the enemy.

Keep awake! Watch at all times. The devil is working against you.
He is walking around like a hungry lion with his mouth open.
He is looking for someone to eat.

I Peter 5:8 NLV

WALKING WITH THE MASTER

When walking with the Master, don't run too far ahead...

Anyone who runs ahead and does not continue
in the teaching of Christ does not have God; whoever continues in
the teaching has both the Father and the Son.

II John 1:9 NIV

...lag too far behind...

Forgetting the past and looking forward to what lies ahead,
I press on to reach the end of the race and receive the heavenly prize
for which God, through Christ Jesus, is calling us.

Philippians 3:13b-14 NLT

...or get distracted by something on the side, or you will soon feel uncomfortable tension on your leash.

...So let us run the race that is before us and never give up.
We should remove from our lives anything that would get in the way
and the sin that so easily holds us back.

Hebrews 12:1b NCV

When the Master puts you on a short leash, it's either to protect you...

Good sense will protect you; understanding will guard you.

Proverbs 2:11 NCV

...or to protect others from you.

Love each other as brothers and sisters. Be tenderhearted,
and keep a humble attitude. Don't repay evil for evil. Don't retaliate with
insults when people insult you. Instead, pay them back with a blessing.
That is what God has called you to do, and he will bless you for it.

I Peter 3:8b-9 NLT

If the Master lengthens your leash, don't abuse the privilege or you'll be put on a short leash again.

A man's wisdom gives him patience; it is to his glory to overlook an offense.

Proverbs 19:11 NIV

The Master will fight your enemies if necessary.

LORD, even when I have trouble all around me,
you will keep me alive. When my enemies are angry,
you will reach down and save me by your power.

Psalm 138:7 NCV

It's a good idea to just completely avoid certain yards.

Run from anything that stimulates youthful lusts. Instead, pursue righteous living, faithfulness, love, and peace. Enjoy the companionship of those who call on the Lord with pure hearts.

II Timothy 2:22 NLT

Keep a humble heart, even towards your enemies.

Do nothing out of rivalry or conceit, but in humility consider
others as more important than yourselves.

Philippians 2:3 HCSB

If you're not humble, you might end up humiliated.

What I'm saying is, If you walk around with your nose in the air,
you're going to end up flat on your face....

Luke 14:11a MSG

If you get hurt along the way, the Master will carry you to safety.

Even to your old age and gray hairs I am he,
I am he who will sustain you. I have made you and I will carry you;
I will sustain you and I will rescue you.

Isaiah 46:4 NIV

At times the Master may walk you through something that seems scary.

But now thus says the LORD, he who created you, O Jacob, he who formed you, O Israel: "Fear not, for I have redeemed you; I have called you by name, you are mine. When you pass through the waters, I will be with you; and through the rivers, they shall not overwhelm you; when you walk through fire you shall not be burned, and the flame shall not consume you."

Isaiah 43:1-2 ESV

In those times, more than ever, let your focus become clear and distractions fade away.

…Take my words to heart. Follow my commands, and you will live…
Look straight ahead, and fix your eyes on what lies before you.
Mark out a straight path for your feet; stay on the safe path.
Don't get sidetracked; keep your feet from following evil.

Proverbs 4:4,25-27 NLT

Remember the Master is with you, and don't be afraid.

Yes, even if I walk through the valley of the shadow of death, I will not
be afraid of anything, because You are with me. You have a walking stick
with which to guide and one with which to help. These comfort me.

Psalm 23:4 NLV

OBEDIENCE

Your ears should always be perked when the Master is speaking.

My son, if you accept my words and store up my commands within you, turning your ear to wisdom and applying your heart to understanding, and if you call out for insight and cry aloud for understanding, and if you look for it as for silver and search for it as for hidden treasure, then you will understand the fear of the LORD and find the knowledge of God. For the LORD gives wisdom, and from his mouth come knowledge and understanding.

Proverbs 2:1-6 NIV

The Master says a lot more to you than you may understand, but He sees how hard you're trying and He loves you for it.

The teaching of your word gives light, so even the simple can understand.
I pant with expectation, longing for your commands.

Psalm 119:130-131 NLT

When you do understand what the Master wants, run to obey His command.

I run in the path of your commands, for you have set my heart free.
Psalm 119:32 NIV

The more time you spend with the Master, the more you'll recognize His voice.

My sheep recognize my voice. I know them, and they follow me.

John 10:27 MSG

If you leave the Master's house and roll around in the dirt, you're going to get dirty.

A good person who gives in to evil is like a muddy spring or a dirty well.

Proverbs 25:26 NCV

When the Master calls your name, come running immediately.

I will instruct you and teach you in the way you should go;
I will counsel you and watch over you. Do not be like the horse
or the mule, which have no understanding but must be controlled
by bit and bridle or they will not come to you.

Psalm 32:8-9 NIV

Pretending like you don't hear the Master doesn't fool Him.

So be careful and do not refuse to listen when God speaks.
Others refused to listen to him when he warned them on earth,
and they did not escape. So it will be worse for us if we refuse
to listen to God who warns us from heaven.

Hebrews 12:25 NCV

It's impossible to hide from the Master.

No one can hide from God. His eyes see everything we do.
We must give an answer to God for what we have done.

Hebrews 4:13 NLV

The Master loves you, even when you've made a mess.

But God showed his great love for us by sending Christ
to die for us while we were still sinners.

Romans 5:8 NLT

When He finds you in a mess, the Master desires to clean you up.

He lifted me out of the slimy pit, out of the mud and mire;
he set my feet on a rock and gave me a firm place to stand.

Psalm 40:2 NIV

Being cleaned up isn't always a pleasant process, but it's better than being left out of the Master's house.

For the moment all discipline seems painful rather than pleasant, but later it yields the peaceful fruit of righteousness to those who have been trained by it.

Hebrews 12:11 ESV

Once you learn how much better it is to be cleaned up by the Master than to stay in your mess, you'll stop hiding and race to leap into the tub.

Repent, then, and turn to God, so that your sins may be wiped out, that times of refreshing may come from the Lord....

Acts 3:19 NIV

It's so much better to just obey the Master the first time and avoid the mess.

His divine power has given us everything required for life
and godliness, through the knowledge of Him who called us by His own
glory and goodness. By these He has given us very great and precious
promises, so that through them you may share in the divine nature,
escaping the corruption that is in the world because of evil desires.

II Peter 1:3-4 HCSB

Even if you're trying to stay clean, it's still a good idea to examine yourself on a regular basis and get rid of any dirt.

My dear people, since God has promised us these things, we should make ourselves clean. We should clean out everything that makes our lives or our spirits dirty. We should try to be altogether holy because we respect God with fear.

II Corinthians 7:1 WE

The Master gives rewards for obedience.

Jesus said, Truly I tell you, there is no one who has given up and left house or brothers or sisters or mother or father or children or lands for My sake and for the Gospel's who will not receive a hundred times as much now in this time--houses and brothers and sisters and mothers and children and lands, with persecutions--and in the age to come, eternal life.

Mark 10:29-30 AMP

LOYALTY

Never let the Master out of your sight and follow Him wherever He goes.

Let us fix our eyes on Jesus, the author and perfecter of our faith....
Hebrews 12:2a NIV

Other people may not understand if the Master is first place in your life, but don't let that deter you.

...We must obey God instead of men!

Acts 5:29b NLV

If you realize that you've been distracted, or have wandered away and lost sight of the Master, go in search of Him.

When you look for me with all your heart, you will find me.
Jeremiah 29:13 NIRV

Find out what the Master is doing and get involved.

For we are God's co-workers.

I Corinthians 3:9a HCSB

Make sure that you are helping and not hindering His work.

We put no obstacle in anyone's way,
so that no fault may be found with our ministry....

II Corinthians 6:3 ESV

The Master has special plans for you; you don't have to try to take someone else's place.

"For I know the plans I have for you," declares the LORD, "plans
to prosper you and not to harm you, plans to give you hope and a future."

Jeremiah 29:11 NIV

The Master's favor will take you places that others can't go.

For the LORD God is a sun and shield; the LORD bestows favor and honor.
No good thing does he withhold from those who walk uprightly.

Psalm 84:11 ESV

STORMS

In a storm, stay as close to the Master as possible.

The LORD is good, a strong refuge when trouble comes.
He is close to those who trust in him....

Nahum 1:7 NLT

If the storm is severe, jump straight into the Master's lap.

The LORD your God is with you, he is mighty to save.
He will take great delight in you, he will quiet you with his love,
he will rejoice over you with singing.

Zephaniah 3:17 NIV

It doesn't matter what time a storm comes, the Master is always on call.

My help comes from the LORD, who made heaven and earth.
He will not let you be defeated. He who guards you never sleeps.

Psalm 121:2-3 NCV

Don't let the storm cause you to run away from the Master.

The seed on the rocky soil represents those who hear the message
and immediately receive it with joy. But since they don't have deep roots,
they don't last long. They fall away as soon as they have problems
or are persecuted for believing God's word.

Matthew 13:20-21 NLT

If you do run away in a storm, the Master will come looking for you.

I will search for my lost ones who strayed away, and I will bring them safely home again. I will bandage the injured and strengthen the weak.

Ezekiel 34:16a NLT

While the Master is looking for you, He'll call on others to pray...

Sebastian!

But the LORD has chosen you to be his own people. He will always take care of you so that everyone will know how great he is. I would be disobeying the LORD if I stopped praying for you!

I Samuel 12:22-23a CEV

...even if they don't know exactly why.

Likewise the Spirit helps us in our weakness. For we
do not know what to pray for as we ought, but the Spirit himself
intercedes for us with groanings too deep for words. And he who
searches hearts knows what is the mind of the Spirit, because the Spirit
intercedes for the saints according to the will of God.

Romans 8:26-27 ESV

GUARDING YOUR TERRITORY

Guard your home vigilantly from the enemy.

Put on all of God's armor so that you will be able to stand firm
against all strategies of the devil. For we are not fighting against
flesh-and-blood enemies, but against evil rulers and authorities
of the unseen world, against mighty powers in this dark world,
and against evil spirits in the heavenly places.

Ephesians 6:11-12 NLT

When the enemy shows up, make enough noise to alert others.

Son of man, I have made you a watchman for the house of Israel;
so hear the word I speak and give them warning from me.

Ezekiel 3:17 NIV

Your mouth is one of your most important weapons against the enemy. If you learn to use it properly, the enemy will be afraid of you.

...take the sword of the Spirit, which is the word of God.
Pray in the Spirit at all times and on every occasion. Stay alert and
be persistent in your prayers for all believers everywhere.

Ephesians 6:17b-18 NLT

Sometimes it's not enough to just stand your ground; you have to chase the enemy off your property.

So let God control you. Fight the devil and he will run away from you.

James 4:7 WE

You can become so skilled at recognizing the enemy that you can sense him while he's still at a distance and be ready for him.

For someone who lives on milk is still an infant
and doesn't know how to do what is right. Solid food is for those who
are mature, who through training have the skill to recognize
the difference between right and wrong.

Hebrews 5:13-14 NLT

MEAL TIME

The Master's food is better than yours.

Your words are so choice, so tasty;
I prefer them to the best home cooking.

Psalm 119:103 MSG

If you sit patiently and attentively, watching the Master, He'll give you food from His table.

When I discovered your words, I devoured them.
They are my joy and my heart's delight, for I bear your name,
O LORD God of Heaven's Armies.

Jeremiah15:16 NLT

You'll enjoy your food more without distractions.

When you pray, you should go into your room and close
the door and pray to your Father who cannot be seen. Your Father can
see what is done in secret, and he will reward you.

Matthew 6:6 NCV

You may find that the only time without distraction is when everyone else is sleeping.

I stay awake all night so I can think about your promises.
Psalm 119:148 NCV

THE NEIGHBORHOOD

The Master wants you to play well with others...

Always be humble and gentle. Be patient with each other,
making allowance for each other's faults because of your love.
Make every effort to keep yourselves united in the Spirit,
binding yourselves together with peace.

Ephesians 4:2-3 NLT

...those who are different than you,

Faith in Christ Jesus is what makes each of you equal
with each other, whether you are a Jew or a Greek,
a slave or a free person, a man or a woman.

Galatians 3:28 CEV

...and even those who aren't nice to you.

But I tell you, love your enemies. Ask God to do good to those who trouble you. In that way you will be sons of your Father in heaven.

Matthew 5:44-45a WE

If your mouth is causing problems, it's your heart that must change.

For out of the overflow of the heart the mouth speaks.
The good man brings good things out of the good stored up in him,
and the evil man brings evil things out of the evil stored up in him.

Matthew 12:34b-35 NIV

The Master is not impressed when you pretend to be nice just because someone else is looking.

...obey your masters in all things. Do not obey just when they are watching you, to gain their favor, but serve them honestly, because you respect the Lord.

Colossians 3:22 NCV

You'll know you are maturing when you are able to walk side by side with others.

But if we live in the light, as God does, we share in life with each other.
And the blood of his Son Jesus washes all our sins away.

I John 1:7 CEV

When you learn to treat others like you should, you can even help The Master lead those who are lost back home.

We were sent to speak for Christ, and God is begging
you to listen to our message. We speak for Christ and sincerely
ask you to make peace with God.

II Corinthians 5:20 CEV

MAN'S BEST FRIEND

The Master delights in you.

For the LORD delights in his people; he crowns the humble with victory.

Psalm 149:4 NLT

The best place to find the hand of the Master is to sit at His feet.

Seek first God's kingdom and what God wants.
Then all your other needs will be met as well.

Matthew 6:33 NCV

The Master wants you to tell Him what you need...

Keep on asking, and you will receive what you ask for. Keep on seeking,
and you will find. Keep on knocking, and the door will be opened to you.
For everyone who asks, receives. Everyone who seeks, finds.
And to everyone who knocks, the door will be opened.

Matthew 7:7-8 NLT

...but He will do even more for you than what you need because He loves you.

God did not keep back his own Son, but he gave him for us.
If God did this, won't he freely give us everything else?

Romans 8:32 CEV

Though the Master wants to take care of your needs, He brought you to His home for relationship.

Even before he made the world, God loved us and chose us in Christ to be holy and without fault in his eyes. God decided in advance to adopt us into his own family by bringing us to himself through Jesus Christ. This is what he wanted to do, and it gave him great pleasure.

Ephesians 1:4-5 NLT

The Master loves to be lavished with love.

Love the Lord your God with all your heart, with all your soul,
with all your mind, and with all your strength.

Mark 12:30 HCSB

Your outward expressions of joy bring pleasure to the Master.

Come, let us sing for joy to the LORD; let us shout aloud
to the Rock of our salvation. Let us come before him with
thanksgiving and extol him with music and song.

Psalm 95:1-2 NIV

You'll even sleep better just knowing you are in the Master's house.

In peace I will both lie down and sleep, for You, Lord, alone make me dwell in safety and confident trust.

Psalm 4:8 AMP

Even then He will take care of your needs.

He will cover you with his feathers. He will shelter you with his wings.
His faithful promises are your armor and protection.

Psalm 91:4 NLT

TRUST

The Master wants to tell you as much as He possibly can...

The Lord shares his plans with those who have respect for him.
He makes his covenant known to them.

Psalm 25:14 NIRV

...but there are *some* things the Master can't tell you yet because you can't handle the anticipation.

There is so much more I want to tell you, but you can't bear it now.

John 16:12 NLT

The Master's absence is unbearable.

There are many rooms in my Father's house.
I wouldn't tell you this, unless it was true. I am going there to prepare
a place for each of you. After I have done this, I will come back
and take you with me. Then we will be together.

John 14:2-3 CEV

Snarling at the Master when you don't like what He's doing can only get you into trouble.

Does the clay dispute with the one who shapes it, saying,
'Stop, you're doing it wrong!' Does the pot exclaim,
'How clumsy can you be?'

Isaiah 45:9b NLT

You can spare yourself a lot of anxiety if you trust the Master more.

You will keep the man in perfect peace whose mind
is kept on You, because he trusts in You.

Isaiah 26:3 NLV

The Master will never abandon you.

I will ask the Father, and he will give you another Helper to be with you forever— the Spirit of truth. The world cannot accept him, because it does not see him or know him. But you know him, because he lives with you and he will be in you. I will not leave you all alone like orphans; I will come back to you.

John 14:16-18 NCV

The more you know the Master and experience His love and faithfulness, the more you'll learn to trust Him.

Lord, those who know you will trust in you.
You have never deserted those who look to you.

Psalm 9:10 NIRV

Always be watching and waiting for the Master to return.

...Christ died only once to take away the sins of many people.
But when he comes again, it will not be to take away sin.
He will come to save everyone who is waiting for him.

Hebrews 9:28 CEV

Behave in such a way that when He returns you can greet Him with ecstatic joy.

For the grace of God that brings salvation has appeared to all men.
It teaches us to say "No" to ungodliness and worldly passions,
and to live self-controlled, upright and godly lives in this present age,
while we wait for the blessed hope—the glorious appearing of our
great God and Savior, Jesus Christ, who gave himself for us to redeem
us from all wickedness and to purify for himself a people
that are his very own, eager to do what is good.

Titus 2:11-14 NIV

Love, Sebastian

Baby Sebastian with his first family ~ Steve & Laura Bennett

Childhood playmates Coda & Sebastian

Sebastian with Jason & Vickie

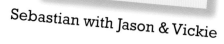

Sebastian's Family & Friends

Birdie (page 79) & Laura

Obie (page 83)

Daddy, Mommy (page 20),
William & Edward (page 55)

Annie (page 81-82)

Duke (page 78)

Toy line-up (page 86)

Snickerdoodle
(page 80)

Jesse & Laura (page 63)

Family Christmas 2007